The obsessive *joy* of AUTISM

JULIA BASCOM

Artwork by ELOU CARROLL

Design by FRANCESCA STURIALE

Jessica Kingsley *Publishers*
London and Philadelphia

First published in 2015
by Jessica Kingsley Publishers
73 Collier Street
London N1 9BE, UK
and
400 Market Street, Suite 400
Philadelphia, PA 19106, USA

www.jkp.com

Library of Congress Cataloging in Publication Data
Bascom, Julia.
The obsessive joy of autism / Julia Bascom.
pages cm
ISBN 978-1-84905-726-4 (alk. paper)
1. Bascom, Julia--Mental health. 2. Autistic people--Biography. 3. Autism--Psychological aspects. 4. Joy. I. Title.
RC553.A88B374 2015
616.85'882--dc23
2014040418

British Library Cataloguing in Publication Data
A CIP catalogue record for this book is available from the British Library

ISBN 978 1 84905 726 4
eISBN 978 1 78450 150 1

Printed and bound in China

For Emily, who promised to build a fort.

I am *autistic*.

I can talk; I talked to myself for a long time before I would talk to

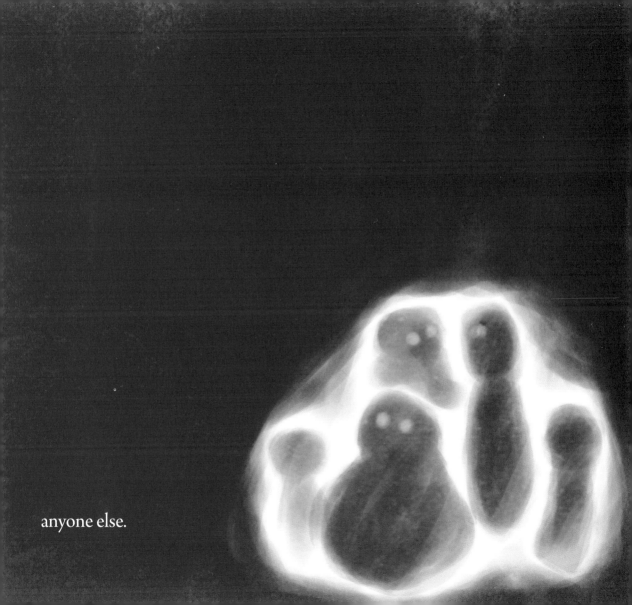

anyone else.

My sensory system is a

PAINFUL MESS,

my grasp on language isn't always the best,
and it takes me quite some time to process social situations.

I cannot yet live on my own
or manage college or relationships successfully.

I can explain, bemoan, and wish away a lot of things about me
and my autism:

my troubles finding the right words
to say what I really mean,
my social processing lag and limits,
my rubbery facial expressions, my anxiety,
my sensory system's dysfunctions,

my brain's tendency to get STUCK

in physical self-destruct mode
and land me
in the ER.

I can complain about the suckiness of being socialized and educated as an autistic and as an outsider, about lack of supports and understanding and always needing to educate.

One of the things about autism is that
a lot of things can make you terribly unhappy
while barely affecting others.

A LOT OF THINGS ARE HARDER.

But some things?

Some things are SO MUCH EASIER.

FLAP

Sometimes being autistic means that you get to be incredibly happy.

And then you get to FLAP.
You get to PERSEVERATE.

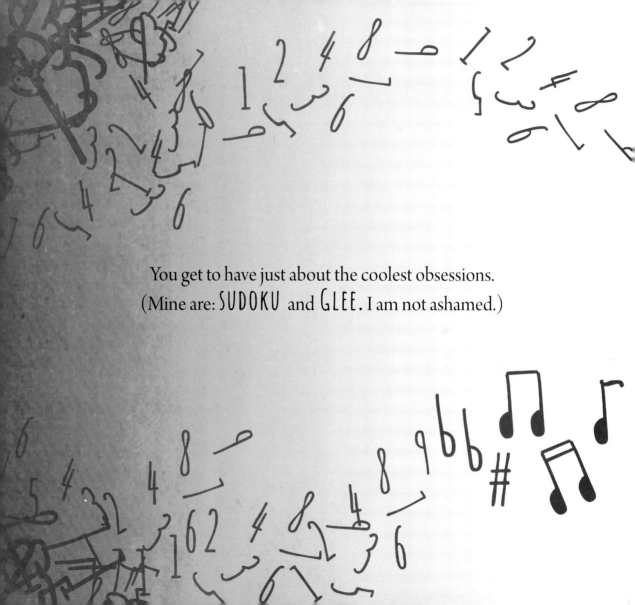

You get to have just about the coolest obsessions.
(Mine are: SUDOKU and GLEE. I am not ashamed.)

Now, maybe you do not understand.
Because "obsession" and even "perseveration"
have specific dictionary and colloquial meanings,
which everyone uses and understands
and which do not even come CLOSE
to describing my relationship with whatever
I'm obsessing on now.

It's not just that I am sitting in my room and

MY HEART IS RACING MY HEART IS RACING

and all I can think about is *Glee*
and all I want to do is read about it
and talk about it
and never go to sleep
because that would take time away from this
and that has been my life for the past few days.

It's not just that I am doing sudokus in my head
or that I find ways to talk about either numbers or *Glee*
in any conversation,
including ones about needing to give a student a sensory break
so he'll stop screaming and throwing things.

(It's not just the association and pressure of shame,
because whenever an autistic person
gets autistically excited about something,
there will be people there to shame and bully them,
and some of us will internalize that shame
and lock away our obsessions
and believe the bullies and let them take away

THIS UNIQUE, UNTRANSLATABLE JOY

and turn it into

SOMETHING DIRTY AND BATTERED.)

It's not any of that.

Those are all things neurotypicals can understand and process.

This goes beyond that.

It's not anything recognized on

THE CONTINUUM OF "NORMAL."

NORMAL NORMAL NORMAL NORMAL NORMAL NORMAL NORMAL NORMAL NORMAL NORMAL NORMAL NORMAL

It's that the experience is so rich.

It's textured, vibrant, and layered.

It exudes .

joy

joy

joy

joy

joy

IT IS A HUG MACHINE FOR MY BRAIN.

It makes my heart pump faster and my mouth twitch back into a smile every few minutes.

I feel like I'm SPARKLING.

Every inch of me is totally engaged in
and powered up by the obsession.

Things are clear.
It is beautiful.
It is perfect.

I flap a lot when I think about *Glee* or when I finish a sudoku puzzle.
I make funny little sounds.

I SPIN. I ROCK. I LAUGH. I AM HAPPY.

Being autistic, to me, means a lot of different things,
but one of the best things is that
I can be *so happy, so enraptured* about things no one else understands and so

wrapped up in my own joy

that not only does it not matter that no one else shares it, but it can become

contagious.

This is the part about autism I can never explain.
This is the part I never want to lose.

Without this part autism is not worth having.

Neurotypical people pity autistics. I pity neurotypicals.
I pity anyone who cannot feel the way that flapping your hands *just so*

AMPLIFIES
everything
you feel *and thrusts it up into the air.*

I pity anyone who doesn't understand

how beautiful the multiples of seven are,

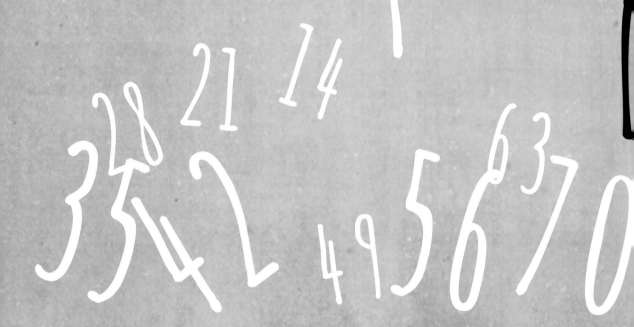

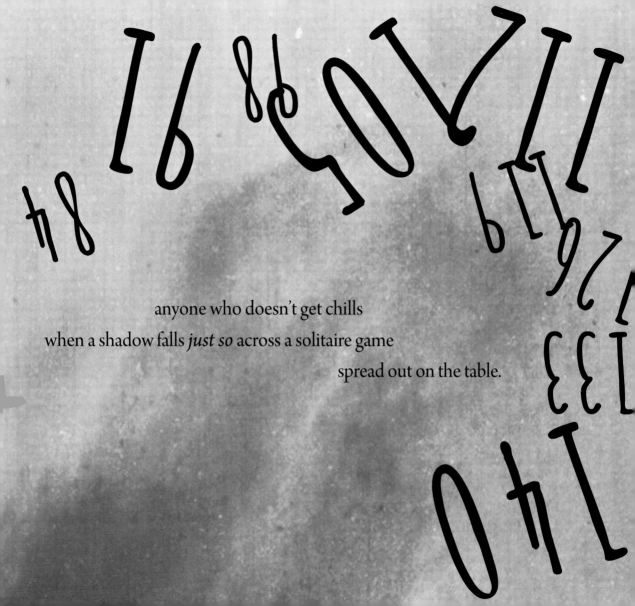

anyone who doesn't get chills

when a shadow falls *just so* across a solitaire game

spread out on the table.

I pity anyone who is so restrained
by what is considered acceptable happiness
that they will never understand when I say that
sometimes being autistic in this world means
walking through a crowd of silently miserable people
and holding your happiness like a secret or a baby,
letting it warm you
as your mind runs on the familiar tracks of an obsession
and lights your way through the day.

IT TAKES A MILLION DIFFERENT

IT TAKES A MILLION DIFFERENT FORMS IT TAKES A MILLION DIFFERENT FORMS IT TAKES A MILLION DIFFERENT FORMS IT TAKES A MILLION DIFFERENT

FORMS.

A boy pacing by himself,
    flapping and humming and laughing.

    An "interest" or obsession that is
        "age-appropriate"—or maybe one that is not.

        A shake of the fingers in front of the eyes,
        a monologue,
            an echolaliated phrase.

All of these things autistic people
are supposed to be ashamed of and stop doing?

They are how we communicate our joy.

If I could change three things about

HOW THE WORLD SEES AUTISM,

they would be these.

That the world would see that we feel joy—sometimes

a joy so intense and private
and all—encompassing

that it eclipses anything the world might feel.

That the world would stop punishing us for our joy,
stop grabbing flapping hands and eliminating interests
that are not "age-appropriate," stop shaming and gas-lighting us
into believing that we are never, and can never be, happy.

And that our joy would be valued in and of itself,

seen as a necessary and beautiful

part of our disability, pursued, and shared.

This is about the **JOY**

So, I guess if I'm trying to explain what an obsession
(and, by necessity, obsessive joy) *means* to me as an autistic person,
I can bring it back to the tired old image of a little professor
cornering an unsuspecting passerby and lecturing them for half an hour.

All too often this encounter is viewed through
the terrified eyes of the unwillingly captive audience.

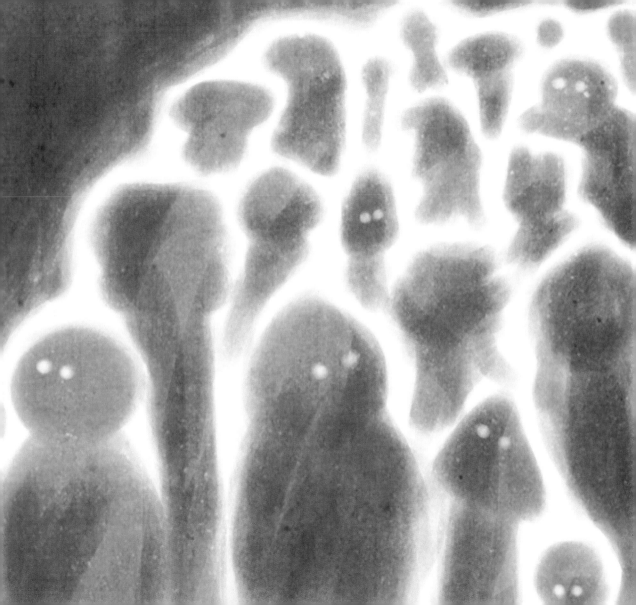

I'd like to invite you to see through the eyes of the lecturer,
who is not so much determined to force their knowledge
into you as they are opened to

A FLOOD OF JOY

JOY JOY

JOY JOY JOY

JOY JOY JOY JOY

JOY JOY JOY JOY JOY

JOY JOY JOY JOY JOY JOY

JOY JOY JOY JOY JOY JOY JOY

JOY JOY JOY JOY JOY JOY JOY JOY

which they cannot contain.

JOY JOY JOY JOY JOY JOY JOY JOY JOY

JOY JOY JOY JOY JOY JOY JOY JOY JOY JOY

JOY JOY JOY JOY JOY JOY JOY JOY JOY JOY JOY

AND WHY WOULD YOU WANT
TO CONTAIN SOMETHING
LIKE THAT?

Note from the Author

When Jessica Kingsley Publishers first approached me about turning *Obsessive Joy* into a book, I was hesitant. I wrote the piece three years ago, and it's not something I've touched since; it said exactly what I needed to then, and it resonated with quite a few people. There's never been a need to find a better explanation. So, of course, looking back now, there are parts I would word differently, things I would change—in the years since I wrote it, I've come to believe even more in boundaries and privacy, to resent a world that insists I rattle off my impairments and medical histories before I am granted an opinion. But in the end, I agreed to have *Obsessive Joy* published in this form because it tells a story about autism that is very rarely told.

Autism, we are told, is hard. And it is. But it's also so much more. And when we talk about autism, we ought to tell the truth. We ought to tell the whole story.

The truth is, my life has a lot of things in it that are hard, difficult, painful, frustrating. I'm told most lives do. But my life also has a lot of love in it, a lot of beauty, a lot of joy. When I twist my fingers or shake the bracelets on my wrist, when I come across a multiple of seven or see a red brick building or ride a train or hear a chord progression open *just so*, everything is perfectly sized and full of light.

If you have an autistic person in your life, look for our joy. Chase that joy. Get obsessed.

We'll see you on the bright side.

Julia Bascom